flipped eye publishing

a storm between fingers

simple words rendered sublime

a storm between fingers

flipped eye publishing limited
www.flippedeye.net

Editing & Selection: Roger Robinson, Jacob Sam-La Rose, Peter Kahn.

This anthology is typeset in Lacuna, a font created by Glashaus Design, and Palatino from Linotype GmbH

ISBN: 1-905233-13-2
ISBN-13: 9781905233137

British Library Cataloguing in Publication Data
A catalogue record for this book is available from the British Library

This project is partially supported by a Community Arts Assistance program grant from the City of Chicago Department of Cultural Affairs and the Illinois Arts Council, a state agency.

Supported by
The National Lottery®
through Arts Council England

ARTS COUNCIL ENGLAND

a storm between fingers

malika's kitchen

Contents

Isle of Dogs afternoon

Home is a houseboat,
nestled uneasily between Canary Wharf,
the Brunswick Arms, the Dome;
we don't bridge the gap.

My life is all maternity
afternoons in a no-work world.
The Thames bank – all dogs, school-holiday children
men with their backs tanned tough as leather –
lager, fags and this surprising weather are no antidote
to apathy; work an unlikely pastime
sometimes, round here.

Some Muslim youths have got a bong up
on the wall, even the girl in a hijab takes a turn.
On the shingle beach below, exposed
now the tide is low, is a bath,
some traffic cones, countless
bottles scattered in the stones.

Over on the grass a lad is walking
his rabbit on a lead
(I have to look twice)
but it's nice now the day has cooled;
the rivulets of sweat coursing down
my arms and legs have dried.

Honeysuckle over the walls
belie the windows adorned
with Union Jacks, West Ham flags;
this is NF country, Isle of Dogs, daytime
TV inertia means an almost-calm presides.
Amongst the racist graffiti, a lamppost's missing
light; it occurs to me these flats
look more beautiful by night.

There's a grudging feeling of live and let live,
of paths that cross but don't touch,
lives lived in boxes, behind glass
folk who don't get out much.
Outside, the ships and boats that pass dance
with the tide whilst Greenwich is only a mile
across the river, but a latte and pastries
world apart. On this side the old guard are
cut off in more ways than one, by a tower;
immigration of the suits and salaries kind,
a sense of community gone.

In the window of an upstairs flat
the birds in a cage, twitter
with Frank Sinatra above
the musty aftertaste of old age.

There are buggies everywhere
as the other mothers and I
share knowing 'mummy' smiles.
My baby found her feet today,
pleased as punch
she won't let them go.
She couldn't know yet
how little any of us belong.

The view is all industrial,
but the Thames glitters like a jewel,
and the sun is out and shining
on an Isle of Dogs afternoon.

migration

I think I hate her now
but hate's too strong.
I am numb; ice held to a wound.
I tell myself I don't love her anymore.

Eighteen, the first time our paths forked:
Finally away from home, I felt her
homesickness in my belly like a stone,
as if it were mine.

Twenty nine: She says why
can't I be happy for her? As tears storm
down both our cheeks and we yell
We're in Durham – the trees outside sickly

orange, unreal. Right
then, I could still feel,
because my mind wouldn't allow me to
grasp she will really go.

But it was there, the violent wrench of days ahead
her children not yet born, our lives stretched
twelve thousand miles apart. It would have been
better if she had cut me, cleanly,

instead of tugging, like intestines
pulled to breaking point.

Being twins, no one ever differentiated us
I answered to her name more often than mine
'til at least the age of twenty five, we have
ridden a see-saw of sharing versus selfishness

Charlotte Ansell

dominance versus giving in,
hating versus loving too long
to let these knots unravel into indifferent miles
with more than oceans to wade across.

We turned thirty-five
today. This loss won't ever heal;
the cost is a life sentence.

Moni-ka-ka-ka.

He says her name like Moni-ka-ka-ka
breaking off from being an aeroplane

she has a faraway smile again, moist eyes
dreaming of babies, fat ones, lots of them

pudgy arms reaching up for her, sticky
kisses and mouthing Mmm Mmm for Mummy

tears that can only be quenched by her,
little ones she doesn't have to give back.

She was always the aspiring housewife,
glamorous hostess, sex kitten, skilled chef

a coffee table you'd be afraid
to put your feet on, banished stains, no mess.

She'd be a vision from the fifties;
dutiful, bringing his slippers after work;

the man, the kids, the house in the suburb,
lipstick flawless, no career but housework.

Impossible to see it in bed-sit land, room
heaped high, mountained junk, magazines

a small clearing on the bed where she sleeps
mould growing on discarded plates and cups

and she'd be always out, flying, grooving
round any room, be-bopping up and down

Charlotte Ansell

bag slung on her back swinging, fag in hand,
the original festival party girl

but she would give up every all-nighter
hang up her whistle and her heels for good

forget the particular haze of dawn
hungry as birds, a chirpy afterglow

leave behind the sweet yeasty bread calling
from the bakery half-way up Brixton Hill

she would never swallow another pill
down a short or re-apply her make-up

if it meant she could be the domestic
queen she carries close to her heart. Life

would be a perfect oasis of calm, waiting
for him to come home, a child on each arm.

What You Need to Do

Go to the woods
and get outside yourself.

If you want to know God,
watch a leaf grow.

The river turns over rock
older than thought and worry.

Face into the wind
and listen as the birds do

what they have always done:
sing for one another.

Hungerford Bridge

Since you jumped
I have wondered
what death was like

On sweltering nights, hay fever attacks,
I awake starved of wind, oxygen scarce
listless, clogged up by a sticky cork, gasping,
gaping mouth working like a fish,
my tongue coated with white spots
where my mouth attempted to keep me alive
and I fight crying, trumpeting my nostrils
with mighty heaves.

Then I think of you.

For three years you have been
submerged
missed your step off the tall red barrier
your stride into air
blinked and you were air walking
feet scissoring with nothing
then
landing like a life raft on the Thames
pinstriped suit ballooned
brief case dislodged
for a moment   time stopped

now every time I walk across Hungerford Bridge
I see you step, land, and balloon

I took a bath the other day
and thought of you
landing.

Portrait

Then
Caribbean intellectual, push in slippers dark as the wooden floors you
lacquered. Khaki long trousers, and white short sleeve shirt jack, with
long strides, slow gait, *why hurry* you always said *life waits for you.* Short
Afro, side parted, kinky. Dreams for houses formed furrows between your
brows. Your nightly absences meant forgotten cinema trips, children and
wife left waiting. Five am door taps, hushed footsteps betrayed by the
crack and snap of floorboards.

Now
Foreign father, sneakers, jeans, and short sleeve shirt, first two buttons
open. Hair, red brown with grey tints, Face lined with years, soft folds of
skin loose at the throat. You are sunken, fragile. The furrows in your brow
are permanent. You live alone. Plan to make it big. Where are the women
now, who squandered your dreams? Wife and children, long gone, across
the seas, your sons walking; long strides, with slow gait, their legacy; *why
hurry?*

Malika Booker

The Maze

1

Absurd Charade

It starts out fun,   then
there is the same dead
end.   The same two women
again.   Walk
another way. Pass
the same women. Meet
the same dead end. Smile,
like you know the way
out.   Turn another corner
another dead   end,
turn back,   it's
the same two women.
Now you feel like
a wasp, hitting itself
over and over
on a glass pane,   knowing
there is a way out
of this maze,
desperate   to find
it. So you pass
the same women   again,
smile   vaguely,
Not fooling anyone.

Maze etiquette

Black iron fence, coated with leaves, a manicured hedge patterned in square blocks, bordering pathways. Peering through the green mesh, to glimpse people moving, see a concrete bench – the maze centre. See the exit sign, right there through the gap but can't get to it. By now the mind plays tricks, I have passed here before. People's words carry though the maze as if next to me, but I am alone on my path. *"lets go left, then right, mummy I wanna go this way, exit, see I am right"*. I hear splatters of Chinese, Italian, German, and Dutch. Imagine they are saying the same things. Nothing here is simple.

Malika Booker

3

Angel of the labyrinth - Saviour of lost souls

I am still
lost in this labyrinth,
when he arrives eyes dancing
mischief, impish smile,
His wings a Jan sport rucksack,
Halo a Nike cap,
his robe an oversized Lakers
t-shirt with khaki combat shorts.
He is easily seven years old.
He stops
in front of me, asks
If I am lost,
tells me follow him.
walks ahead
looking back
to see if I am
still there,
his expanding cheeks
entice me to smile back at him.
He leads me out like a lamb
leading a shepherd.
At the entrance I say thanks
blink and he is gone.
The gatekeeper tells me
I am not the first,
he has been saving
lost souls all afternoon.

L-vis (dis)covers the blues

one night, after dinner fight
grades down like his attitude
L-vis huffed out the bungalow
like an asthmatic, tears and snot;
a sweet and sour dessert in his mouth.

hopped the bus he was warned against,
the one that crossed the side of the city
Javaughn, Durrel and most of the guys
on the team lived. he'd never been invited.

last stop; a street he'd never seen,
a strip of currency exchanges, hair
salons, storefront churches, corner
store conversations like foreign
languages, mothers' stern voices
corralling children home. metal carts
carrying groceries, laundry, or scraps
of construction, depending
on who was pushing.

he gazed down side streets
filled with men in front of tools and cars and coolers,
music twisting out factory issued stereos like yarn
caught in the trees and pigtails of little girls riding
pink-streamered bicycles on the sidewalk,
white tires rolling over chalk rainbows.

                                        and then he saw

                      fenced-in black-
        top playground   hands beat bricks
to a beat   headz bent
& nodding   talk fast
drum roll   body part base
line, stories   over boom
bap   mouth
music, words
picked up   like passes
        ran with   however long
           one's breath will carry them

Posing

in a full length mirror
on the sliding closet door
of the bedroom i share
with my brother, in the town-
home my mother rents in the suburbs,

an X-cap tilts / over my shaved head
like an unplayable pinball machine.

nose still too big
for my face. chin hairs,
i'd call a goatee,
struggle for articulation.

                         i look hard

i am shirtless
in a Raiders Starter™ jacket,
belt strung thru loops of 38/34 jeans,
pools of denim wade
at my Tim-less ankles.

every muscle in my body
wishes it were Bigger.

Kevin Coval

Faded

the stylist at Michael Anthony Salon
has got no idea what a fresh cut is.

a step, a bowl, a bald wall
straight lined over the ears
like my head wuz a topographically diverse region n shit.

for prom i wanted to get a peace sign shaved in the back.
i went to Quick Cuts™ in the strip mall on Dundee.
the barber was frail n divorced, dirty blond
thirtyish somethin, her fingers smelled
like Kools. she just put a restraining order
on her second husband. said she'd give it a try.

                    when i got home
                    n looked in the mirror

            pac man.

        a Mercedes
        hood ornament.

            no fuckin
                    peace.

Candy Bar Brownies

when she couldn't hold food down
I would walk by bathroom door
listen to the quiet she would try to make

she would come out
grab mixing bowls, baking pans
preheat oven so warm
I'd turn the space heater off

she was not accurate with her steps
used counter top like banister
with spoon in the other hand

bought her a Kitchen Aid last Christmas
she never learned to use it
her brownies wouldn't taste the same
if they weren't some sweat in them
she used to say

sit down
I tell her

I don't enjoy sitting
she replies

Collecting

She must have shown me a dazzling gem
once, then my slippery fingers were caught
in the drawer looking for more, until she
died and the whole cabinet disappeared.
But a diamond, a gold chain I kept quiet.

Other people did not have jewels like hers.
Mum didn't, hers were pretend gold, plastic
or things seen in local stores, on other necks;
jumbled in an old biscuit tin, not grand
or holding stories of before I was born.

I learnt of who she loved, and who loved her,
and even so kept their diamonds and gold.
Of cinnamon markets, corralled green seas,
eating apricots in spring, long train rides,
what began as her mother's, her brother's.

She knew I loved them and wanted precious
things too; toying longingly, admiring
them dripping around my neck, swimming loose
on my wrist, fingers. I would try to slip one
away, but her searching eye clawed it back.

I learnt that grandma used to be richer,
her jewellery real gold and scarves cool silk,
that each little box, velvet lined or silver
embossed, had a story found piece by
piece with each secret guilty opening.

Halfway round the world is too far

I wish
I could sit in your garden
with nothing much to say.
Long, empty time,
with nothing to do.
You would just be there,
occasionally top up the teapot,
pick me sun-bruised berries to taste,
put out sandwiches and juice.
You would look at me the way you do,
that's all.

Because here,
in this clunky radio-blasting city
I spend too many days wandering,
and I'm afraid,
I won't get where I am supposed to,
or be something to somebody,
or stamp my mark somewhere
on the pock-marked pavement.

Here in your garden,
you and I,
as perennial as the last twenty years,
opened doors to each other,
sat in our gardens at all times
of the day and night:
when the night was dead quiet and secret,
whispering under a blanket,
when we were sun-drunk,
lying limp on warm grass dozing.
I wish

Cath Drake

I could just sit in your garden
with nothing much to say.
Dissolve into the background
of pot plants and tomato vines,
see you look at me now again.

Attention to Detail

She bends her puffy fingers over so
each nail, professionally-filed, natural-glossed
catches the white light
surrounding her
in the hospital.
She pulls at the front of her white gown
like a child tugging a mother's coat
checks it's fastened tightly at the back
ensuring her dignity
is preserved.
Before she's wheeled
into theatre
she reapplies plum-cherry lipstick,
draws in eyebrows
where they once were
kohls her eyes. Prays
the eyeliner is waterproof.

Loud

It's in my father's eyes, the sunken
sockets. The static laughter lines.
The lips pressed tight,
the strong square back to her.
His red and white beer can crashes
down on the veneer table
my mum has just polished.
They are not whispering.
He picks up the can again,
his head thrust backward.
The hollow sipping sound.
This time the can sounds different
lighter, as he crashes
it down. I push the door fully open
from its crack. It's the way they stop
mid flow, like musical statues.
He gets up, grabs his coat.
I dare you to drive in that state
She says to the slamming front door.
His figure is mangled
through the textured glass.

Talking Drum Machine
for the African/Caribbean/British/American Diaspora

"...Bass for your face, London..."
- Flavor Flav, Public Enemy

Transatlantic black
America sails across
the pond to squeeze the throat
of the Queen; hypnotise
her children's *(bling, bling...)*
minds into madness.

The blind lead,
disoriented, rudderless,
compass cracked and spinning,
the offspring of amnesiacs; memory,
a white smudged black slate.
Imperialism's bastard
teenagers acting up, airing
a storm of dirty laundry
on radio waves.

(...s.o.s...)

England's elderly neck
caves beneath the sneakers of American
adolescents (trainers, tracksuits,
trashmouth), their wastebands
bulging, cold steel tucked
in their voice boxes,
broadcasting.

The Knowledge of Knowing

She wished it were deeper, something
like the insightful way he deconstructs
Christianity's imperialistic urge, or
the delicious curve his brushstroke
makes on the largest batik in the gallery.

Instead it's the line the side of his neck
makes while he's driving, she
in the backseat, the veil of his eyes
in the rearview mirror slanted
in the direction of her disaster,

the arch of his eyebrows a lit match
to the petrol tank of her body, the messy
slosh of her wanting, wanting familiar
as the smell of lovers five years gone,
and the trigger it pulls on the Deringer of memory.

His hands, now resting in the right curve
of his steering wheel, she imagines spinning her
into liquid and steam, something frothy
as cream on his overused bed, but she knows:

It's just a fantasy, really, and the distance between
desire and doing is a kite tangled in the trees of emotion.

TOO MUCH HIP HOP
For the dying gatekeepers

You won't hear this
cuz you don't go to poetry readings
stage plays or youth slams
don't ride public transportation
you don't wake before 3pm
work a day job or make phone calls

You only move when the beat drops
draped in album cover art
slammin blunt gut fingernails on MPC
fondling the fader, imagining yourself Prometheus
a six-corner legend
with a marquee name

giant

in your cave
thirsty desperate
shrouded figures
keep you disillusioned
singeing mic cords
Newports stay burnin
til sunrise

You only know how to listen
to dusty soul brothers on rotation
the way they plead for understanding

You resent the waking world
Think them not strong enough
for your chaos and the stress
worn thick like goose down

My Academic Lunch

To begin
we ordered veggie chili
and an ambrosia salad

killed white corporate
animal cannibal psychos
pealed back the layers
of social strata until she recognised
the waiter from a party the previous night

She thinks they may have made out

We blasted overseas conflicts like skeet pigeons
ordered buffalo chicken sandwiches
while the bones of great leaders
on our t-shirts sat still

our food arrived we ate
then picked our teeth
rubbed our bellies
as the bus boy cleaned
off our table

Dropped

What do you do
when water turns gasoline.
Grass is ground glass.
Leaves, lobbed grenades.

When answers are over-
cooked questions. Hard
to swallow. Stuck
in your teeth.

What do you do
when sleep is sandpaper.
Sunrise, Agent Orange.
Hope, a mouth of buckshot.

When "I'll always love you"
becomes "I no longer do."
Always,
a dropped mirror.

Pinch

This is how you know
which ones we are
                    - Elizabeth Alexander from, "Orange"

I.
Pinching is supposed
to tell us if we are
dreaming. My arm has twelve welts

from my two finger vise.
Or are they tattoos?
Bug bites? Purple punch stamps?

II.
I passed out at the doctor's
office last summer. The waking
was dream-like. Eery. Near-

death. Visited places
over-grown
with wiry weeds.

Whirling *wom wom wom*
juggled me like slugging
wave tops, like I was single sock

in spin cycle.
It seemed more real
than now.

                    How do we know when a pinch is real?
How do we know
which one we are?

What's Left

Here's what's left:

Two marbles staring
like glass eyes crossed.

Five faded script cards—
birthdays and Valentine's.

4 torn up photos,
smiles split.

1 fake flower,
wilted.

1 silver necklace,
tarnished.

1 Lindt milk chocolate bar,
uneaten.

1 letter with stomping script
like a bull, betrayed.

A shoebox filled with everything
reminding her of us.

A box top,
re-secured.

Peter Kahn

Fracture

The weight
of their own bones

breaking causes cattle
to die at the slaughterhouse.

Hanging from hind legs,

spines snap.

My bones are light:
resistance serves your erection,
insistent   your hands
grip my throat.

In your bedroom,
no one hears the siren
trapped by your fingers.
Neck snapped back.

Stem of a lily,

breath escaping.

Stigmata

It's the blood that screams, always the blood.

Dirty silver caught the rays of a harsh
Texan sun as you handed me the flask
of wine across the car seat. I swallowed

deeply, bound to you. Riding shotgun, I
gazed out at the faded polaroid towns
marking our progress across America.

We skirted digitally still cities
sharp in the abstinence of faith. Strip mall
shoppers were your congregation, until

celebrity upgraded you to football
stadiums and 35% income brackets.
Hallelujah seekers formed your choir

as you placed your hands upon
the foreheads of the irredeemable, stoking
the fire of belief, healed them – like

you healed me, out on the back lot
of Wal-Mart, years ago. I focused
on the apex of pole and tent in the

dingy partial light of my sky, seen
over the shoulder of a soldier of
Christ. My blood screamed then too,

we both heard it, brazen and loud staining
the crotch of my blue cotton panties. I wore
Wednesday on Sunday. You struck with a zealot's fire

and the conviction of the right hand of
fellowship. It was through you that God
worked. You saved me, making me speak

in the indecipherable purity of tongues.

My belly remained barren, virgin, as
the father, the son and the holy ghost
resided in my flesh at their leisure.

Whole, I abided as your handmaiden,
servant of your needs, walking behind you
and proselytising in your footsteps.

But now my boots mock me from the corner,
and blood seeps through the pristine white tube
socks tied around the soles of my feet.

Your mouth, ugly in its struggle to pull
air in, to rebuke this new thing between
us, accuses. Fear rests in your eyes, slithers

around your heart and casts me out a
tarnished augur. My palms leave red splotches,
potato prints against waxed linoleum,

as I crawl toward the jangling sound of
wire hangers pinging against a stainless
steel bar you pull three piece suits from.

You have dropped to your knees, kneeling
amongst meagre piles of useless belongings, it's
the first time I have seen you really pray.

Beseeching God to correct his blasphemy.

I know I will be able to buy the
house next door and build a chapel, appoint
a priest for my ministry, endure the

doubts of skeptics and the pedestals of
believers, but I won't be able to
keep you, my Saviour, because I AM

no longer Mary; and you can't see me
as Jesus. Your role, you yell heavenward,
but tell that to my bleeding stigmatas.

Donna Lamar

Waiting

I say I came for you.
You slap your hands together and
look at me, sharpening the distance
between us on opposite sides of the
world, in a 2001 convertible Saab.

2 years... How can you be waiting
on a person if they don't know, you say,
straining toward me looking for answers...
you knew I say... "you taught me about love"
slips from between your lips before
you say, I've gotta go.

4 days later you call to tell me that it's
sad, my waiting. No one's worth that,
life's too short. Sad, you repeat, before
you say you gotta know when to let go.

Later that night, sleepless, I think the only
difference between my waiting and yours
is that you had me for the four years you
waited for her to come back. What else
is there to say?

Train ride

Blue scorched horizon watches
me travel Colombo to Kandy

Sea whispers breezes into twisted
green valleys carved upon hillsides

Elbow anchored on brown splintered
ledge nudges the morning air

The engine's steamed heat infects each carriage
swelling ankles, affects the sales of ice-teas.

We slow to take a turn; a ribbon of children
offering garlands of smiles run by my window,

shouting Singhalese arpeggios
with breathless punctuation

their laughter travelling along
the hips of mother's country.

Jetty

Anchored, washed and splintered feet
firm through silt and sediment,
years of fishing-rod stories cast into the night;
water swallows time slow.

Lizards scurry my surface like a stranger's touch
when only distant houses watch, I creak
and mourn those dismantled by hurricanes
now flotsam on ocean's skin.

New hands trace my damp oak
lifelines in watered green, bone to beam
he takes out a small box, hugs her close
like a lifejacket and whispers their future.

It hums through my beams
as diamonds sparkle in the salty water.

Moms Mabley Reads Her Lifeline of War

I was born the year Teddy
shot up San Jaun Hill.
Puerto Rico became property
to abuse cuz coloreds who speak
Spanish is still negroes in the hearts
of Gringos.

The year my Bonnie broke
my water, Jack left me,
and the boys came back
from the War to end all Wars.
The next year White men
without the consent of congress
waged war on Negroes
killed or maimed thousands
in 1919's Red Summer.

I was doing my last Broadway show
when Kamikazes flew to Hawaii
to blow peace out the water.
When our boys led the last dying
Jew to a freedom no Negro had
known in America, I was slinging
tears from folks congregating
in chitlin circuit dives.

By the time the first corn fed
kid dropped dead in Korean mud,
I was dubbed "funniest woman
in the world.

Round the time flames rose like falling tears
because the King of love and civil rights
laid out with a bullet in his head,
I was recording at the Playboy Club.

Since then I've seen more chiren kiss
the face of God in Vietnam or come home
pieces of their bodies left in a rice paddy
or their minds stuck on a dead girl's face.

So I's want you to keep protesting.
You may not end this war
but you'd be right to use your right.
That's what they say they send poor
boys and girls to fight for.

Now, I can't promise you won't go to jail
but I guarantee you will not go to hell.

Blind Man's Gold

I almost broke my ankles to prove I could dunk,
spending my baby's bath-hour, girlfriend's picnic time
and mother's church and Sunday lunch marathon's

playing 3-on-3 half-court games to 11, staying
until I won. I traded summers for the sound of a ball
dropping clean through a net, leaving work early

camouflaged in civilian apparel. Winning was
an antidote to my apathy. I made temples
from London parks, invoking every backboard.

The chant of the ball was a call
to prayer. The sound of freedom.
I stored my dreams inside each pass.

Replica

I remember my first camera
in which I stored the portrait of my life
– a window to nostalgia.

It became a map to the best parts of me
shown only to the ones I love.
This time machine of Technicolor memories;

it kept what was hidden to my subconscious.
There is a version of me that always
smiles at the barrel of a lens.

The last replica sat with my father,
an African carving of a man,
whose heart was gentle as his voice.

I had seen more of him in pictures
than in person, his image preserved by negatives
that held his heart but not his voice.

The lens caught him looking
into my daughter's eyes,
love leaking out the sides of his smile.

Sleeve-Hearts

Have you ever given of yourself freely?
Generous.
Charity.
Would have called you Chastity,
Till I found out the truth.
See, our hearts pump while intertwined
With the shirt thread that we use as the veins
We inject our heroin of attention into.
I know you're an addict, baby
Because I am too.
Hopefully,
You don't get your heart stepped on.
Unfortunately,
I've already committed that crime.
On stages, where
We both do open heart surgery.
You, with song.
I, with rhyme.
We used to be the only people
On parents' telephones.
Now,
I never speak
Unless there is a speaker near.
I never hear you
Unless there is vibrato involved.
It seems the more we open up,
The more chances there are
To have our hearts ripped out
From chest cavities.
Wearin' it on the arm hurts
More than tattoo pricklings.

I know you know I know but
Why
Are you here now?
Why
Did you let him hurt you?
Why
Do you let them dictate who you are?
They are not God,
They are only audience members.
They are only guilt by-standards.

Aqua Soul

Well-seasoned meat marinates in sea, salt. Emotions
tenderised by immersion in holy waters.
Toxic mind finds quiet release in its turbulence
   I bake in dry sand
lay sideways like a crab. Caress
close my eyes, whisper heart. Offerings become
prayers of thanksgiving and celebration.
Dance lacy white ruffles to wave on turquoise skirt.

Flutter fingers over raging body 'til limbs levitate above my head
like sorceress.
Conjure She
rock me in way no man can. Sun

seaweed-soaked salt baths in seabed
wash deepest dirt stains off essence like baptism within
ecstatic trans-Atlantic. Dip
my forefinger into the healing tip of Her open mouth.

Warm waves crash sweetly
remind me of a familiar refrain
the oldest song ever written:
Cool me down   to simmer
in surprise bursts
like a busted fire hydrant
running wild in 100 degree heat

Idea Of Ancestry (I/II)

Seasons flower then fade
freedom. Captured release
in dreamtime.
Purge problematic planet
hurdle crippling cosmos crisis
with ease of Joanna Hayes.

Future-addict-born-slave.
Crave survival
like spicy savour of simmering jollof
scented fog.
Thick aroma meanders.
Maggi seasoned living
sticks to white walls
peppered with decades of grease-stained-growing
pains

Tomorrow is a marinade of blood spilled
yesterdays. Descendants
inwardly seethe to slow burn.
Angry vapours rise toward heaven like ethereal prayers.
Curdle passions.
Survivors choke on ferment sea
salt tears. Clear eyes
Holy Ghost baptism by fire
triggers rebirth.

Idea of Ancestry (II/II)

Ageless body
Eternal mind
Timeless spirit
Shackled to *his story*
like unbreakable metal clamp
fixed to right foot.
Skeleton lock me to stolen land.
Grounded
Naija-caged-bird
on verge of extinction.

Unsure why I return.
Didn't learn
enough about colour of suffering
redemption singing
inherited deprivation.
Buried alive before conception
six feet deep.

Poverty beckons promise,
remember indigenous song
liberate imprisoned native tongue.
Shriek of maternal cry echoes in deaf ears.
Summon first generation
resurrect breathless dreams from dead sleep
like Lazarus.

Ugochi Nwaogwugwu

Flesh

Flesh is like dough.
Knead it. Let it yield
beneath your fingers.
Brand it with your palm.
Leave a scar.

Paolo (a sea shanty)

He had eyes the colour of black pebbles on the beach
Limpid black and shiny wet as pebbles on the beach

And his smile was white as the bleached insides of seashells
Pearly white as the bleached insides of seashells

And his nose was the proud peak of an Andalucian mountain
Proud and imposing as the rolling Andalucian mountains

And his forehead rose to meet his hairline
Like the blue Costa sea met the blue Costa sky

And his lips were wide with promises of a night not spent alone
Lips wide and plump as blood oranges, full of promises

And his manly arms were open as he welcomed me to stay
And he smelled of warm grapes and sea-salt and welcome

And for one perfect moment, underneath that perfect sun,
with that perfect man, I was perfectly in love

Then I sat at Paolo's bar and ordered my first drink

Denrele Ogunwa

Fag Ends

We're sucking the last smoky breath
from the fag end of a dying millennium
watching re-runs of bad movies
we can't afford to be elsewhere
so broke we're scrabbling for old butts
to make a decent cigarette
blowing bubbles in our cheap wine
to make champagne

We make toasts, promises
you'll make more money
I'll finish 'the book'
these repeated resolutions
have become our mantra
multiple Hail Marys, penance
for another year wantonly wasted

I test 2000 on my tongue
let it roll out like factory fresh fags
It tastes hopeful, rounded
full of good things coming
perfect as a smoke ring
new and dizzying
as that first nicotine high

and we hang on to those shimmering Os
working them onto our fingers
like wedding bands
pledging our vows
against a backdrop of midnight
revels and wet confetti

In the distance
Big Ben's donging
the grey sky's flashing
with impatient fireworks
and as I peer out the window
I can feel time running out
like a cigarette burning

Denrele Ogunwa

Common/wealth

at the Commonwealth Institute, London

Without wheels their boy bodies are eloquent
in the cool air, tightly coiled springs
that jump and whirl and oscillate effortlessly

the same way boasts slip off
the roofs of their mouths like clay shingles.
Each move is demonstrated

with familiar ease, every element of motion
executed like a locksmith decodes
a knot, then the ringing chatter settles

like a dropped coin,

the expectant clatter of skateboards
rises then turns to air, flared jeans
lift, then fall, as though for a second

they had lungs, and the boys are mounted.
The first boy's feet propel him
towards idle boasts and after graceful

coasting, he launches himself, a raised flag;
his flight is jerky yet hopeful, like a plea
in a tongue he hasn't mastered the rolling of.

A la Carte

Absorbed in the transparent music
of clinking glasses, I am slashed
back to the mundane by a waiter

handing me a menu ex cathedra
then slinking away as silently
as an espadrille-shoed ghost

Around me my seven companions
delve feverishly into the textual
mysteries of the folded card, fondling

its ridged paper expectantly
as they debate: chicken, fish or lamb?
I bear a crippled smile as I open

my pleated gift knowing I will be stumped
as I always am by the ambiguity
of culinary lingo; does seared tuna

mean cooked on high heat for three
or five minutes, on one or both sides?
This is why I rarely go to restaurants;

for the same reason I censor the news:
What makes an Iraqi victim unfortunate
and an American one tragic? What makes

Somoza an OK guy, and Castro a vile man?
Is it the same ghost that decides that
Che was a guerrilla, and the lobster is done?

Nii Ayikwei Parkes

Red String

Sister Joyce is celebrating
Jesus in a G-String.

Hollas, whoops and hallelujahs;
dancehall makes way for divinity.

They're singing real loud
like a favoured Mary J tune;

praying for sins
they've yet to commit.

They're bringing all they've got,
voices failing

as they sway in time
arms flailing,

as she eyes a too high heel,
a skin design peeping from a chest:

where his word is
tattooed on a heart.

Her eyes shut, fingers crossed, legs closed,
oblivious to the ladder of her fishnets,

she fingers the red string of her bible,
marks a Psalm before snapping it shut.

Til she's singing again, real loud
and he's smiling, saying come as you are

to the fisher of men
who makes fish clean

Maida

Walking on Maida dirt, the colour of unripe plums;
the red Bauxite my mother couldn't wait to escape
strays into my sandals, lingers
settles under the arch of my foot.

A woman's eyes shadow me: Behind
the roll of my hips my bottom
sits atop my legs, perches
on the exaggerated dip of my back.

Shoulders, wide and upright, counter
balance heavy cleavage, walking
filled with 'self surance'; upturned
milk-bottle calves power forward

You're Kitty's daughter she calls;

her words, full of certainty, bowl me
over from their distance. Here in this
place of sameness, poverty and heat

she is certain I belong
to a woman who left 43 years ago
wearing this same shape, I wear well.

Janett Plummer

Song for Angela

My mother is a twin,
or should I say my mother
is part of a twin.
My grandmother told me that
they used to sing together.
She showed me a picture
of them winning prizes.
What people didn't know
is that they actually
had the same voice, she said,
and together,
they had a haunting texture
that would impress the judges
time after time.

As a child
I remember sleepy nights
in small theatres,
where they'd raise
their voices in chorus,
their afros perfectly global,
framing their faces like halos.
Their dashiki robes,
like the cloth equivalents
of stained glass windows
of the Sistine chapel,
as they belted out
their folk tune chorus.

When I was a teen
one morning I saw them cooking
an Easter weekend brunch.

As they diced and chopped
the smell of fresh thyme
and baking fish
hung in the air like mist.
I heard them start a tune together in key,
without any signals,
not even a look,
their afros now straightened out
into razor sharp bobs,
falling at their cheeks
as thick and fluid as Indian ink,
their dashikis abandoned
for batik wraps, folk tunes replaced
by hymns with calypso flavour.
They sang their duet to God in unison
for three hours, till the food
was ready to be served.

I saw them sing again,
together in that room
when Angela,
my mother's twin,
her face serene
as a newborn baby's
lay in bed.
My mother's hair cropped
short and grey with age.
Angela's hair short
through chemo
and grey with age,
holding my mother's hand,
saying she felt no pain
saying she had no regrets
saying goodbye to everyone,
then they sang:

Roger Robinson

"*Then sings my soul my saviour god to thee*
How great thou art, how great thou art
Then sings my soul, my saviour god to thee
How great thou art, how"
then she squeezed my mothers hand
stopping her short,
and my mother looked at her
and Angela whispered, she's ready,
and pushed her head back
into her pillow
as if to get comfy for her journey
as she smiled and closed her eyes.

Today this Easter morning
my mother starts cooking brunch,
and she's trying to keep a tune
past the cracks in her throat,
and smiling through her tears
she stops, she starts again
trying to keep her tune
past the tears, palming them
off her cheeks, she stops...
She starts again and I join in
to sing Angela's part.

Lab

For Maria

1

It was the year we used the biology lab. We entered to the gassy smell
of the Bunsen burners, the anatomical charts and the lacquered, dark
brown surface of the tables. The thing that I remembered most was the
row of jars, descending in height, that contained babies. Not dolls, or
models, but real children, the colour of pickled onions slid into jars, like
fish to be gazed at.

2

That year Mark told me that his girlfriend was pregnant, and that they
wanted to use my house because both my parents worked. We left school
at lunchtime to meet his girlfriend; by the time we got to my house she
was wiping tears in her school shirt. I lit the kitchen stove and boiled some
Guinness whilst Mark put the brown, twenty-dollar pill on the table. We
all sat staring at it for ten silent minutes. She said she couldn't do it and
he began to beg her to. I reheated the Guinness and brought it back to
the table, and that time she drank it down and lay down in the bedroom.
Mark and I tried to watch some TV. She screamed out and ran to the toilet.
Mark grabbed my hand as she screamed for the next ten minutes then she
stopped. She walked out dazed and stumbled to the couch.

3

I wiped the spilled sticky brown Guinness from the stove, scrubbed the
bloodstains from the toilet bowl and changed the sheets soaked with
sweat in the bedroom. After an hour they called a taxi. I looked at her
through the tinted window. Crouched like a punished child on the back
seat. The gray waxed shine of the car. Mark's worried eyes, the smell of
the exhaust and the disappearing speck.

Roger Robinson

The New Puppies

When I visit my mother at Christmas
she always has new puppies.
Brown and white furballs, with tiny slit eyes
short legs and floppy ears. They're like clones
of last year's puppies and the year before's.

Now I'm an adult my age has bought rank.
I'm allowed to sit royally and shout
commands at my young cousins and stray kids
too poor to have a good Christmas elsewhere.
They shine my shoes and bring me orange juice.

They in turn try to get the puppies
to fetch thrown balls and twigs in the backyard,
but the puppies only respond to bowls of milk
and a tickled stomach, as they roll over
catatonic with the joy of touch.

At night I stay up late with my mother
making traditional Christmas snacks
as night rain hits the tin roof like applause.
She wakes each one of the seven children
individually at different times. She gives each one

a special snack and a hug and makes them swear
not to tell the others; so they all wake with the glow
of a favourite child. I ask her what has happened
to all the old puppies and she gives
various reasons like: a bigger dog killed them

or they ran away, or they were crushed
by a reversing car. She says this without
a dimming in her eyes or a lilt of sorrow
in her voice, like someone used to losing
things and having them replaced.

September Rain

September and her cups of tea
Sweet chai, dreams
And these mid November realities

Sipping mugfuls of the stuff
Watching the condensation on the window grow
I dash out two eyes and look down

To the street below
See the passing strangers' sorrow
In a city that all too easily lets go

Leaves turn from green to brown
Summer left, now Autumn has come around
Leaving us standing still, in a season of change

Another song left unpenned and unsung
Though the world does not miss this
Continues to spin on her axis

Another book left unthumbed and untouched
The dust seals the pages deftly down the spine
Though promised inside were words like wine

And I remember you, though you do not recognise me
As the saxophone wailed, the singer paled and the women railed
You measured the moment in your scale of niceties

September and her cups of tea
Sweet chai, dreams and these
Mid November realities

Algebra

For OPRF High School, Chicago

I'm 29 in a high school maths lesson.
I've had dreams like this. Nightmares.

The teacher speaks a different language,
a vocabulary of numbers. Inconsistent graphs.
Tests. Slopes. $x+y. y=3x-2$. I daydream that

maybe there's music in these numbers.
If x were a tree and y were a sound,
negative a over b might equal

the Chicagoan wind, a bow string of air
making leaves sing. I imagine black notes
rolling down a woman's cheek.

Last night, I saw a woman cry,
stunned by the strength of her own words
scored on a page, a flood of memory.

There are numbers everywhere.
The teacher gives two methods of solving
equations: substitution or elimination.

The woman that cried has three siblings.
She, the only one that kept her mother's Xmas bow.
She hasn't seen her mother for seven months.

Immigration equals a blank wall with no doors,
dividing her family, crowned by an eagle
looking down from a nest of barbed wire.

The teacher points to the board and asks
is this consistent? A student asks if this is the point
of intersection. The woman that shed tears

doesn't know if she'll see her mother again,
and there's a music in everything: in chalk
tapping out problems and solutions on a board,

in layers of chalk dust falling on a classroom floor
like passing minutes, in school bells marking
a lesson's end, in tears coaxed into words,

and where there's music, there's beauty.

Jacob Sam-La Rose

Things That Could Happen

1.
She swoons, falls into his arms
and they live together happily ever after.

2.
She kisses him: the restaurant applauds.

3.
There's a pin-drop silence. She turns
the knife in her hand, slowly.

4.
His heart bursts in his mouth before he can say the words.
It splatters the table, ruins her dress, and she never forgives him.

5.
He's interrupted by a handsome man from another table
who asks if he can cut in. She accepts, of course,
and waltzes off to an orchestra of cutlery, side-plates,
strummed napkins and warm bread. He seethes, turns bald
and tells the story to every man he meets.

6.
She falls in love with the waiter.

7.
She falls in love with the waitress.

8.
She starts by saying that she's quitting the country,
that there's nothing in London to keep her.

9.
He loses his voice, has to write it all down.
She spills a glass of wine, the ink blurs and swims
across the page. *I'm sorry* she says, and he nods,
his eyes turning to crystal.

10.
They laugh.

11.
They have passionate sex in the single toilet.
Outside, a lengthening queue tuts and frets.
Someone presses their ear to the door.

12.
She doesn't believe him.

13.
They have 3 children. Some nights, she tells them
(again) how their father won her heart
over chicken gyoza and ebi katsu.
Whenever he hears this, something in him rises
like a bull-chested spinnaker.

14.
Her mobile rings. The moment falls, like a crumb,
to the napkin in her lap. She brushes it away.

15.
He learns a new language – says it in French or Swahili.
She's mightily impressed, but doesn't understand.

16.
She chokes on a noodle. The tips of her fingers turn blue
as she fights for breath, and fails. Later, he learns to love
the bite of alcohol and numbs his tongue with ice.

Jacob Sam-La Rose

17.
She chokes on a noodle. He Heimlichs her.
She sees him in a different light,
as he dabs the sparkling sputum
from her lips.

18.
He watches the way she eats
and thinks better of saying anything.

19.
Before he can speak, she leans across the table,
fingers barely touching the corners of his mouth,
and says *I know, already. I know.*

Ymir

In Norse mythology, Ymir was a giant, murdered and dismembered to create heaven and earth.

Imagine you are him. His arms and breath are yours,
and one long night, while sleeping, you are pulled apart,
torn into pieces like confetti thrown to the wind. You become

a world. One eye always shining while the other sleeps.
Your skull is full of air, your flesh becomes the ground
that others walk upon, your bones are broken and remade

as mountains, teeth dug out for rocks, and for a while, you think
you might wake up and pull yourself together, rise and walk
away, but you no longer own your feet and toes. You learn

to speak without a tongue. When you sigh, your breath
makes leaves and branches sing, but no one listens to
your voice. Tell me, how do you feel? Imagine you are him.

Your heart still beats, but it's called something else, now.
You dream in colours, black and sky blue.
In time, you'll forget your own name.

Jacob Sam-La Rose

Save The Children

-    Last week, Sharrieff asked me who I was
before lately.
Paused   told him
I always been a good kid
didn't get the best grades
but was always a sweet kid.
Always been a good kid
sweet kid, you know...

-    12 or 13 years ago
on trips back from Wela's house
the car stuffed with talk
of Ethiopians
how *they* don't have McDonald's
french fries.
My father never told me
where Ethiopia was
until that night.
Huddled around our 20" RCA
he pointed at the melon
stomach of a boy with skin
thin like wrinkled homework
paper, digging through landfill like a sandbox.
His eyes, big, looked
like my brother's.

-   Next morning, when mother isn't looking
I climb a kitchen stool.
Take bread
colour of my palms.
Toast it till it looks
like the back of my hand.
With an "Our Father" I put it
in a sandwich baggie
gently place it
in the garbage
hoping my landfill
is his sandbox.

Christina Santana

My Father's Brother

I.
They dared his aim.
Bet a pack of cigarettes
he couldn't crack
the old jibaro's window
three houses down.

He pulled back
a tan leather pouch
tied to bacon-thick rubber bands.

Marbles: ammo.
Let go.

My father's brother,
Junior, killed a man
with a slingshot.

II.
Now, he paces across Viequez.
Gathers coconuts
from orphaned trees,
sells them for a dollar.

Only left his business to visit
his mother's funeral back in St. Thomas
where he gave me a t-shirt he made--
"*Se Venden Cocos.*"

I tell him he'd make more money
if he sold the shirts.

　　He says nothing--
　　teeth rotten
　　from letting go.

White Narcissi

Yet again, we wake from the same dream.
You are staring at yourself in a lake
surrounded by white narcissi

while I look back at you
as a reflection in Stygian waters.
All you can see are the parts of your face

as they separate from each other.
First, the eyes move apart, right
from left, ears following

each other across the lake
like pollen expelled from a swollen bud.
Next, the mouth splits into

a muffled scream that repeats around us
as we hold onto each other, shaking
as our bones turn into rocks.

Leather Belt

I buckle this belt around my waist.
It feels like letter O, round and tight.
As I walk to the bedroom mirror, I see
the face of Lilith who looks back at me.
I listen to a voice who tells me to cover
my ears from the hissing that grows louder.
When I touch the leather skin,
each brass eyelet stares back at me.
When I open my eyes, I see myself
walking from an orchard garden
that smells of rotten apples.
And later when I unfasten this buckle,
I stare at my reflection as the belt falls
and then slithers back into Adam's ribs.

Insects

I ask my niece why she messed up
our kitchen wall with green doodle.
She points to a squashed
bottle of washing-up liquid
in the pedestal bin.

I had turned over the next page
of Baudelaire's *Fleurs du Mal*
when I realised our house was too quiet
for a six-year-old playing downstairs.
Now I am asking her why.

That summer, I watched ants
stumble across the threshold of our house.
In straight military lines,
they carried grains of demerara sugar
to a colony in the garden.

Gran stopped these angry insects
from marching into our home.
She squirted detergent on the outside step.
In the afternoon, black bodies lay
like full stops on the ground.

Now I am asking my niece why
in the middle of the kitchen.
I hate flies, she shouts.
I wanted to drown them.
I strike her cheek.

Now I know how those fragile bodies felt
as they fell into that sticky fluid.
Delicate dipterans flapped
until torn thoraces stuck to green liquid.
My niece asks me why but I can't answer.

Denise Saul

The Last Compass Point

His hands remember fighting for food
searching through bones for loved ones
cupping Papa's chest tightly to ease the bleeding
until his heart stopped

waving goodbye to Sierra Leone.
It is the first time Mohammed has seen snow.
He spreads sun-blackened hands on the white blanket.
A cold freedom comes from this movement.

Three weeks ago, he arrived to a locked room
two immigration officers, one pale interpreter
and Mohammed, the last compass point, facing east
facing fear. He knelt as the trinity talked,

unable to clutch at their words.
Ungloved, his hands can survive
a freezing British welcome at Christmas.
Those hands, outstretched, searching for Allah.

Aubergine Angels

Inside Old Street Station,
I meet my Waterloo.

Aubergine afro's primed
shining and armed. Wrestling

my gaze from brief-cases,
city zombies sockets;

the sweat on the back
of broad builders' tee-shirts;

a small boy's arms running
with ice-cream; seeing smells

from a bacon sarnie,
come out the happy mouth

of a homeless woman.
I'm arrested! The sight,

the light of the grander dark
haloes, moving me up

and out. So I exit
to City Road behind

young Black boys. Black Angels.

Heart and Feet

My toes curl. I watch for her breath,
smell death. On the ward bed,
heart-red stain at her mouth,
she is still. I see her toenails, red

like mine. I did them last night,
let me go out with style, she said.
The screen's a flat red line,
a lone tone, the nurse turns off

my heart. It slips out my feet
stains a smudge on the clean floor.
Can I ask the nurse to fix this?
You gave me my heart to love with,

my feet to move through the world.
A ring of coins around your feet,
a toll for the gate,
soft red earth and leaves at her heels.

Halloween in Winter

At recess, we'd layer into snowpants,
hooded jackets, stringed mittens,
double-scarf our faces and slip over
costumes, loose on de-wintered bodies

during classroom hours, that clung to our snowsuits
as we pushed outside to explore snowbanks.
These costumes followed us through photographs,
princesses, wizards, us sweating under catsuits

made to rival Andrew Lloyd Webber
during all-night sewing sessions,
they passed through our family to end
in charity shop bags and other families' photos.

They twinge our memories of night falling early like the snow
as our moms kept vigil by sand salted roads,
blowing breath into hands, stomping feet,
holding kleenex for runny noses and we,

with glow-in-the-dark bags heavy with candy,
navigated iced sidewalks, barrelled through valleys
made from shovelled paths to ring doorbells
screaming trick or treat, singing, laughing.

CASH

Oh how you rattled down your dusty track,
Audiences hungry for the songed jail time
That only came after they wore you down,
Replaced your picks with pills and stage collapses.

Your body became Joseph's coat:
A patchwork of pieces as you pushed on,
Your jaw unhinged after a 200 a year concert habit
That spanned 3 times your brother's life –
His last day the first day you started to write, his bible
        silenced by a woodcutters blade
While you Huck Finned. There was no Red Riding Hood
        hidden in his chest
And fish never tasted the same after that day.

But still, the man comes around to turn childish lyrics
Into platinum records earned to the rhythm of wheels on pavement
Day-night-day-night-day-night-day-night
Passing like county border signs.

Your mom said you had the calling – piano man, rough guitars,
The gravel of your cotton farm upbringing deep in your throat,
Your thorn-pricked fingers desperately clinging to the gospel,
You tried to do for her and him and Him;

Your band of mechanics were more used to tuning cars than guitars,
But the lights of arenas still laid tracks to money signs
        instead of Baptist revivals
So your family got everything they needed except what they needed
When you left them for Gomorrah, the fear of trumpet sounds forgotten.

Lost in floods of studio lights, crowds clapping time
And blondes and brunettes who would have been virgins
If it was before Elvis instead of after;
Left all the songs you wanted to sing abandoned.

Was it your God who sent you a rock-rap legend to save you,
Pull you from your cave, sweating and shaking,
The empty bottles piled in yesterday's trash?

The den of vipers and over-bright teeth he sent you into
Propelled you back into your Sunny days
Your hands slicing through strings, shoes polished
The once forbidden fruit helping you to stand
And extinguish the fire ring that once contained you.

The stories captured in grainy recordings, undiscovered sessions,
Family produced celluloid, phoenix fired you back
         into the memories of another generation,
Imprinted photographs - the sheen of black,
White jackets, thin ties, rock-a-billy hair, captured
         moments that made your life
Ring true again, a man who could take impossible lyrics
         and make them his own.

Heather Taylor

voodou

lemon juice man marry peach cobbler woman her faithful   him
impractical   moved last young dip in they house   keepin *widower* lie
straight him locked wife in basement   her stopped eatin   17 months
later   foundt her rottin   him went fishin   feelin heartsunken-ed   him
expired   17 days later
maker dont like unbeautiful

"they" over-sight or my "sensitivity"

me respondin to the January 31, 2006 issue of the London
Guardian's article
- What (London's) Top Writers Say Every Child Should Read

blk folk must
dont write.
maybe read
dark materials. but nothin
we cud sit-chew-weight
aloud on page
cud ever be
im-po-tent.

g. brooks may lucked up
doodled Pul-itzer prize work
but us bean eaters unworthy
a *must*-read listin.

blk folk must
dont in-tel-lect,
but we do compute
even nigger hangers believe
in the fire next time.

n thats cool's cool
cause i know
bein **blk**

ery child dont give
no-fuck bout white boy-
witches fitted up in dresses
who straddle brooms.

avery r. young

Hurricane Katrina poem no. 5
neighborly

1.

yesterday mz. ida rang on door
sayin blockclub collectin old clothes
shoes can *goods* n holla
when I get my donation together

stinky azz nigga solicitin
change of whateva sort
her tell him *damn shame*
folk out her really need shit
n all you wanna do is quarterbeg people
n be high

2.

    not too long befo Katrina blew nawleans
dry   her screamin to *down on luck* daughter
that sonnuvabitch steal too much
to stay here

as grandbaby tantrumed
fo daddy ... her hot air
deflated him ego

    bread all him had to offer

                                fuck sara lee

crumbs don't pay rent

3.

    today we drivin donation
expedition to church
at red light stop
brother come up windexin windshield

her blast
i aint givin yo black azz nothing
back awaaaaaaaaay from the truck

turn to me say
you don't know if its piss
or what these niggas squirt
on the goddamn window

i pull
dollar outta me pocket
her yank it
swear   *you like bush*

ready to give money
to any n erybody in the world
but cant take care of yo own

i tell her
but
him is

avery r. young

Malika Says...

In Guyana during the late seventies, huge billboards populated the highways with inspirational slogans for the nation. My favourite one was 'together we aspire, together we achieve'. I also loved the Trinidadian saying taken from a popular Calypso song 'All ah we ah one family.' Little did I know that these two quotes would form the basis of a writing collective.

Malika's Kitchen began in my bedroom in Brixton, London in August 2001. We kicked off the first session with one writer, Roger Robinson and myself. Over the next three years, Malika's Kitchen grew under the leadership of myself, Roger Robinson and Jacob Sam-La Rose, and it became an international community of writers when Peter Kahn, an early member of Malika's Kitchen (who cited the Kitchen as one of the reasons for extending his sabbatical in England by a year) moved back to Chicago and started a Chicago branch of the organization.

We now have annual international exchanges. In October, Kitchen representatives are selected to travel from London to Chicago to teach, perform, and cement ties with their Chicagoan peers. In June, Chicago poets come to London. Incredible.

This book represents five years of Malika's Kitchen and features most of the writers who have taken part in workshops with the collective during this time, both in Chicago and London. It is a testimony to the power of the collective in a climate where it's difficult for the individual writer to get their work acknowledged by mainstream poetry publishers. The Kitchen represents a healthy approach to the practice of writing; it is a legacy of our existence.

Malika's Kitchen is a space where writers can develop and learn their craft in a supportive environment. It gives writers access to tools and peer support and enables them to access the literary establishment. Our ethos is that there is always room to improve or develop your craft no matter who you are. The exchange between writers with different voices feeds our writing practice, creating a sense of collaborative competition. We learn from and share work with our peers. We push ourselves forward and in doing so we push each other.

Malika's Kitchen would like to thank:

Roger Robinson, Jacob Sam La Rose and Nii Ayikwei Parkes for tirelessly giving blood to collate and edit this anthology; Peter Kahn and Sifundo for holding the fort and implementing new systems, which enabled us to continue growing; Janett Plummer, Nick Makoha, Denise Saul, Patricia Foster and Sundra Laurence for their hard work; Spread the Word and Stratford Circus for their amazing help and assistance over the last two years; and all the guest poets who have given their free time to lead our sessions and all the writers who have been a part of the Malika Kitchen's Family.

Author Biographies

CHARLOTTE ANSELL lives on a Dutch barge in East London and has been a performance poet for several years. Currently concentrating on being a mummy more than a poet, her work is intensely personal, vibrant and alive. Her lines contain pain, passion and truth. Her first collection 'You Were for the Poem' was published by flipped eye – her second is due out in 2007.

MIKE BARBER is a member of the Chicago branch of Malika's Kitchen.

MALIKA BOOKER, principal founder of Malika's Kitchen, is a writer and performer whose work spans literature, education and cross-arts. She has represented British writing internationally, both independently and with the British Council including the Slovenia (City of Women Festival), Italy, the US, Holland and Switzerland. Malika is best known for her writing, and performances of, intimate and engaging character monologues and poetry, which beautifully capture the contradictions and passions of modern living and transform personal insight into universal appreciation.

KEVIN COVAL is the author of Slingshots (A Hip-Hop Poetica). His writing has appeared in The Spoken Word Revolution (Source Books), Total Chaos (Basic Civitas), Chicago Tribune, Crab Orchard Review, Make Magazine, four times on HBO's Def Poetry Jam, and can be heard regularly on Chicago Public Radio. Founder of The Chicago Teen Poetry Festival, Louder Than A Bomb, Coval is the Artistic Director of Young Chicago Authors and Curator of the Chicago Hip-Hop Theater Festival.
(www.melekyonin.com)

CATH DRAKE has earnt most of her living from writing and communications. She specialised in environmental issues in her native Australia for about eight years where she won awards for her writing. Her work included everything from radio programmes, to newspapers and magazines, nature trails, pamphlets and larger publications. She now works in the press office of a children's charity and runs writing workshops at Centerprise Literature Development Project in Dalston.

PATRICIA FOSTER is a writer, performer, dancer, and educationalist described as "...a gem storyteller of the London poetry scene..." and "... a writer at the top of her tree... ". She has performed poetry and theatre at notable venues across

London. She has also toured and read at numerous literary festivals, events and universities within the UK, Europe, New York and Chicago. Patricia has appeared on Sky TV, as well as live UK and Dutch radio. She has also collaborated with UK Jazz musicians and producers and is currently a presenter on 'The Art Of Words Poets Show', Solar Radio.

KRISTA FRANKLIN is a poet and collagist from Dayton, OH who currently works and lives in Chicago, IL. Her poems have been published in, and her collages presented on, the covers of books, CDs, and print and web magazines including: leadbelly by Tyehimba Jess, (Verse Press), Gravity U.S.A. by Jacqueline Jones LaMon (Quercus Press), nocturnes 2: (re)view of the literary arts, Warpland, Obsidian III, semantikon.com, and milkmag.org. Some of her poems also appeared in Greg Tate's Midnight Lightning: Jimi Hendrix and The Black Experience (Lawrence Books), and in the anthologies The Bust Guide to the New Girl Order and Bum Rush The Page. She is also a Cave Canem alum. (www.kristafranklin.com)

Named one of the most influential people in Chicago under the age of 30 by URChicago Magazine, IDRIS GOODWIN is regarded as one of the hardest working artists in the midwest. Idris is the co-founder of the Hermit Arts Collective, an independent production team producing multimedia performances throughout the city and region. Idris is a frequent guest lecturer, hip hop performer and writing workshop facilitator at prestigious universities, small colleges and progressive institutions across the nation. Idris has been featured in numerous Chicago publications including the Chicago Tribune, Chicago Sun-Times, Chicago Reader, and Chicago Magazine. (www.idrisgoodwin.com/)

Founder of the Chicago branch of Malika's Kitchen, PETER KAHN is a former social worker and high school English teacher who is currently the Spoken Word Poetry and Black Literature Educator, and Project Coordinator in a Chicago area district where he works with students ages 10 through 18. He is the founder of one of the largest Spoken Word Clubs in the country and co-founder of the Inner-London Teen Poetry Slam. His poems have been published in The Moonwort Review, X Magazine and Crest. Peter has performed in various venues in London, Leeds, and Chicago, and was a featured speaker at the 2005 National Council of Teachers of English annual convention.

AMANDA KLONSKY is a Chicago based writer and educator. Amanda teaches poetry and literacy to incarcerated girls at the Cook County Juvenile Detention Center. (www.threadofdevelopment.org)

DONNA LAMAR is an emerging filmmaker making the transition from the world of commercial production. She's an American who resides in London but has spent the last eight years of her life living in Amsterdam and travelling Europe. It is the combination of a European and American aesthetic that informs her work. She's been actively interested in writing for most of her life and specifically in poetry for the last six. Her interest lies in the spaces that exist between actions, words and memory.

SUNDRA LAWRENCE teaches poetry from residencies in Arvon, Yorkshire, to schools in Tower Hamlets. She has performed in a range of venues nationally and internationally. Sundra's work has been broadcast on BBC 2 and radio, and is published in numerous anthologies. Starchild (2003) is her first mini-collection. Sundra lives in North West London.

TONI ASANTE LIGHTFOOT is a native of Washington, DC living in exile in Chicago. She is a teacher, poet, activist and is currently working on a biography of commedienne Jackie "Moms" Mabley. Lightfoot's work can be seen in numerous online journals as well as in Warpland: the journal of Chicago State University. Several of her poems have been anthologized in Role Call, 360 Degrees: A revolution of Black poets, Beyond the Frontier: African-American poets for the 21st century, Cabin Fever, the Cave Canem II, III, and IV collections of the writers' retreat, and Hand Made Fire-Malika's Kitchen Chicago. Lightfoot is the editor of Dream of a Word: A Tia Chucha Press Anthology. As a member and co-founder of The Modern Urban Griots, she co-wrote and directed the poetry plays "Everything I Never Told You Became a Poem" and "Jazz, Wine, and Poetry: An almost love story"

NICHOLAS MAKOHA is a charismatic poet and educationalist who has performed internationally and around the UK including the Royal Festival Hall, Green Room and the Ideas Foundation. A charismatic performer and a part-time mentor to teenagers through the NESTA Ignite programme, Nick's writing explores the ambiguities and contradictions of life, love and relationships through thought-provoking poetry and a searing delivery. (www.nickmakoha.com)

SHARRIEFF MUHAMMAD is a writer who found literacy in Hip-Hop. Upon reading "Bomb the Suburbs" (William Upski Wimsatt), he realized that he can do way more with his education in the culture of hip-hop than simply be an industry clone. He dug deep into the literary side of music/art/inspiration. Poetry called him when he discovered the Chicago open mic scene starting with Young Chicago Authors' hosted open mic "WordWide:Wordplay". Through the Chicago open mic scene, he found himself as an emcee, writer, and performer.

UGOCHI NWAOGWUGWU is an international singing sensation who has been performing her original style of song and word poetics since she began her musical journey. Known in her hometown best for her refined storytelling and songwriting ability as well as the technique and song style she has been known to dub "vocal harmonics," Ugochi's style of spoken word has been fused with her unique singing ability in order to generate a more powerful word sound attraction. A former rapper, turned poet, gone singer, Ugochi has become extremely versatile and creative with the range of music she is able to perform.

DENRELE OGUNWA writes about love, lust, life and other sexually transmitted diseases. Both a published and performance poet, she has performed at Apples & Snakes, Express Excess, Pure Poetry, Speakeasy and other leading poetry venues. She also does the odd poetry workshop with extremely talented teenage poets. She lives in London with her large CD and book collections and has a shoe fetish to rival Imelda Marcos'.

NII AYIKWEI PARKES is a London-based Ghanaian writer and editor and author of three chapbooks; eyes of a boy, lips of a man, M is for Madrigal and shorter. (www.niiparkes.com)

JANETT PLUMMER is the holder of the 2005 Gwendolyn Brooks annual black writers award for open mic poetry. She has been published in PUR magazine and anthologies including 'Flowers on a Shoestring' and teaches poetry and creative writing to children and adults. Janett is the founder of Inspired Word - a women's writing and positive mental health organisation. Her writing is evocative and richly soaked in narrative.

One of the founders of Malika's Kitchen, ROGER ROBINSON makes music, words, performances, recordings and combinations of these things, and was selected by Decibel as one of 50 writers who have influenced the black-British writing canon over the past 50 years. His short stories and poems (Adventures in 3D, Suitcase) have been read internationally at venues and institutions such as the Helsinki Museum of Modern Art and at the New Jersey Performance Arts Center. Roger Robinson and his band The Easy Rockers were presented at the 2005 Sonar Festival in Barcelona. Robinson participated in in the British Festival Of Visual Theatre with his one man shows (Letter from My Father's Brother, Prohibition and Shadow Boxer) created with support from Apples and Snakes and the London Arts Board. His debut album (Illclectica) was released in May 2005 by Altered Vibes recordings.

ANJAN SAHA is a London based writer, musician and arts consultant. He has led on projects and trained at the Independent Theatre Council, Pandit Ram Sahai Foundation and Momentum Arts and was the decibel co-ordinator for

East England. He has written and performed three critically acclaimed shows; 'Mathematics of Rain', 'Tales from the Cooking Pot' and most recently 'Lost Luggage: the art of travelling lightly'.

Well known for intimately detailed and finely crafted poetry, JACOB SAM-LA ROSE has been described as "the backbone of the London poetry scene". Poet, writer, literature in education consultant and performer, his programme of international appearances has taken him as far afield as the Museum of Contemporary Art in Helsinki, Chicago State University, Mylos Theatre (Greece), the Center of Contemporary Art in Glasgow, and London's Queen Elizabeth Hall, as well as a range of more conventional poetry and spoken word venues. Jacob is the artistic director of the London Teenage Poetry Slam, as well as a number of other creative writing and youth poetry initiatives and community projects. His chapbook – 'Communion' [Mouthmark, 2006] – won the Poetry Book Society Pamphlet choice for 2006. (www.jsamlarose.com)

CHRISTINA SANTANA is a 19-year-old Spoken Word poet and educator from Oak Park, Illinois. She was a finalist in the 2004 Chicago Teen Poetry Slam (Louder Than a Bomb). Christina is known for her insights into urban life, references to her Puerto Rican heritage, and her charismatic stage presence.

DENISE SAUL is a poet and fiction writer from south London who has performed at a variety of literary events. As a poet, Denise's pen makes intuitive and yet surprising leaps and bold associations to conjure up vivid imagery which explores everyday themes. Denise has a MA in English: issues in 20th century literature and is currently working on her first collection of poems. She is a former recipient of the George Viner Trust award for her journalistic work and has previously worked as an editor for business publications. Denise is currently researching literature that focuses on black and Jewish writers.

SIFUNDO is award-winning writer she has appeared on BBC radio and television and her poems have been described as 'exquisitely framed pictures'. An inspiring educator, she is Zimbabwean by birth and her name in Ndebele aptly means a beautiful lesson.

DOROTHEA SMARTT is of Barbadian heritage. Dubbed 'Brit-born Bajan international' [Kamau Brathwaithe], her work receives critical attention in Britain, Europe, the Caribbean, and the USA. A poet and live artist, her most recent commission took her to Houston, Texas to work with the community of the historic Project Row Houses. Her poetry collection "Connecting Medium" [Peepal Tree Press, 2001] contains a Forward Poetry Prize 'highly commended poem'. She is currently working toward a second full collection, while a mini-collection, on Lancaster's 'Sambo's Grave', is due in 2007.

Canadian writer, performer and educator HEATHER TAYLOR has been published throughout Europe and North America. In October, her first full poetry collection, 'Horizon & Back', was published by Tall-Lighthouse books. "Taylor writes passionate, hard-won poems, using words honed with razor wire to reveal the bright ice & bone beneath things." – Todd Swift. (www. heathertaylor.co.uk)

avery r. young has been a staple in the spoken word community since 1996. His style of writing, singing and performance is labelled "Sunday Mornin' Jook-Joint." His blend of spoken word, song, jazz, gospel and chant distinguishes him from any other performance artist on the scene today. His work as a teaching artist and mentor for schools and community organizations has made him not only an artist but also advocate for such social dilemmas like HIV, domestic violence and education reform. avery has appeared and work has been featured at The Museum of Contemporary Art, House of Blues, BET, WGN Morning News, MTV, VH1, Kevin's Room 2, The Hip Hop Theatre Festival, Dance Africa, Lalapollza, Wordstock, A New World Reveal-A-Solution, Denizen Kane, New Skool Poetics, World Can't Wait and Taste of Chicago.